Teeth Are Not For Biting

By

Phalan Taylor

<u>JOURNAL JOY</u>

An Imprint of Journal Joy Publishers

www.thejournaljoy.com

Copyright © 2021 by Phalan Taylor

An *Imprint* of Journal Joy *Publishers*

All rights reserved. Printed in the United States of America. No part of this book may be reproduced, distributed, or transmitted in any form or by any means, without the prior written permission of the author, except in the case of brief quotations embodied in critical reviews and certain other noncommercial uses permitted by copyright law.

For information on publishing, contact Journal Joy at Info@thejournaljoy.com.

www.thejournaljoy.com

Summary: Teeth Are Not For Biting brings awareness to the reality that sometimes biting happens. A colorful book to help children remember that Teeth Are Not For Biting; but Eating. A must have in all bookshelves.

ISBN: 978-1-7361688-6-8

Edited by: Riel Felice

Pictures by: Ahva Henderson

First paperback edition, 2021

DEDICATION

Dedication: To the little guy in Sassafras Class who inspired the research that produced this book.

Deep in the jungle lived an alligator who loved to jam with his monkey friends.

The music excited the alligator so much that he began to dance and jump around. He was so happy that he could not think of the words to express his feelings, so...

SNAP!

He tried to bite one of his monkey friends. The little monkey held out his hand and said, "STOP! Teeth are not for biting!"

The alligator walked away. He felt sad because he had almost hurt his friend.

Later that day, the monkeys were looking for a place to rest their bodies. They called out to the alligator, "Lay down with us." But the alligator still wanted to play.

His friends tried to help him rest his body when...

SNAP!

He tried to bite another one of his friends. The little monkey held out his hand and said, "STOP! Teeth are not for biting."

The alligator felt sad again. He didn't want to hurt his friends.

After rest time and a snack, the alligator's teeth were feeling funny. He still wanted something to chew on, but just before he could lean in to bite, one of his monkey friends said, "STOP! We do not bite our friends. They don't like it and it hurts."

"Oh, teeth are not for biting!" said the alligator. "Well, what are they for?" he asked.

"We use our teeth for food," answered all the little monkeys.

From that day forward, the alligator used words to tell the monkeys if he was excited or tired, or if his teeth felt funny. He only used his teeth for food.

Phalan Taylor

Waddies.services@gmail.com

I wrote this story after doing some light research on why children bite. There was a three-year-old in my 2014 preschool class who would bite multiple times throughout the day. The book demonstrates some scenarios of why children bite, according to my research, and provides a solution toward the end that helps the biter and his or her peers.

My co-teacher and I actually taught the children in the class to hold up their hands and say to the biter, "STOP!!! Teeth are not for biting," when he tried to bite them. It worked! Reading this story, encouraging the biter to think before reacting, and providing the children with the proper way to react to the biter's behavior helped the child to stop biting.